From The Beginning To The End

By:

Josephine Brooks-Clark

From The Beginning To The End

By:

Josephine Brooks-Clark

Copyright@2014
All Rights Reserved
Printed in The United States of America

Published By:

ABM Publications
A division of Andrew Bills Ministries, Inc.
PO Box 6811, Orange, CA 92863
www.abmpublications.com

ISBN: 978-1-931820-32-5

All scripture quotations, unless otherwise indicated are taken from The King James Version 1977, Thomas Nelson Publishing and the New International Version 1984. International Bible Society. They are used by permission, with All Rights Reserved.

DEDICATION TO:

All of my grandchildren and great grandchildren

Kevin Jamel,

Eric

Glenn Jr

Krea

Melanie

R'hesia

Anton

Cory

Great grand's

Christian and Michael

TABLE OF CONTENTS

	Autobiography	1
	Brief Synopsis	5
1	Beginning To The End	7
2	How They Met	9
3	Beginning Of Their Family	15
4	Stick-Up Time	19
5	What A Turn Around It Is	23
6	Beginning Of The Worse	27
7	A Mark V111 Lincoln Family Reunion	31
8	Rudy's Lab Results	35
9	Quotes Of Rudy After Waking Up	41
10	Weather Predictions	43
11	The Start Of Something New	51
12	The Handwriting On The Wall	55
13	Rudy's Death	59
14	Josie's New Life	65
15	Special Scriptures & Photos	67

MIRACLES, MIRACLES, AND MIRACLES ARE HAPPENING:

Autobiography:

Josephine Brooks-Clark

My name is Josephine Clark; my friends call me Josie or dimples. Just want to start with when she was a little girl; she always wanted to do things out of the ordinary. She had a twin brother that was born first, she was born about 45 minutes later. When the doctor came into recovery room, lying on the table was Josephine.

The biggest inspiration in her life was their mother, concerning miracles; she taught the children how to believe in God that anything impossible with man is possible with God. Mom taught them how to fast and pray concerning the special needs that only God the

JOSEPHINE CLARK

Father will perform.

She always read books when all of other children were outside playing. As she got older, and started to school she wanted to play basketball, football, roller skate, climbing trees whatever she felt like doing that was fun. Growing up in a house with 6 girls and 4 boys was a lot of fun. On week days they ate beans and corn bread, Saturdays was fish and on Sundays was chicken. They did not have a farm, but father raised chickens, that was ordered from Chicago, Illinois. They had to walk to school and to church. By the time she started high school was when she realized that she wanted more out of life than what she was experiencing. She wanted to be a Mathematician, then a lawyer and then a school teacher. Which one was she? A Special Need Teacher, of which she loved very much.

This one particular time when an accident happened, their oldest sister was living in Germany. Her husband came home for lunch, but on his way returning to work had an accident. An 18 wheeler ran into him head on; the brother-in-law remained in a coma for approximately two or three months. The doctors stated he will not be able walk or talk. This is where their mother stepped into picture.

Their mom called all of the children together to explain what took place, she stated it is now time for the family to go on a three days fast and pray for your sister husband. Their mom always expressed if it is God's will, Bliss, the brother in law will come out of the coma. Praise the father after three days Bliss began to come out of the comas. Years after working with him, Shirl took good care of Bliss, made him go to therapy, walk every day and taught him how to feed himself. Praise God, since then Bliss has recovered all the way and now has two sons and working on a regular job every day. WHAT A MIRACLE!

After graduating from high school, Josie moved to Chicago Illinois and lived with her oldest sister, Shirl. That is when she met Rudy Clark. Life began to change as they started their journey down the road as husband and wife.

Through the years and as you read from the beginning to the end, you will see how the God they served was always there for them. Josie lived in Huntsville, Alabama for ten years before she decided to move to Moreno Valley, California, where her daughter, Valorie and family live. Josie has been a widow for 8 years now after a marriage of 40 years. Born into this marriage are two daughters, Felecia Clark-Harris and Valorie Clark-Baker, where each has four children, and there are eight grand and two great grand.

She decided to return to school online to complete her education. She first attended AIU online and then started attending Colorado Technical University. She will complete this degree in August 2013, which is the second Masters, and then planning to move to California to pursue her career, hopefully as a retail manager that comes in to make changes in any business, regarding their training manual.

It's a funny thing that happens regarding one particular grandchild, Glenn Jr. It's as if Rudy was alive, the grand did not spend a lot of time with him, but it's strange to know some of his mannerism, the way he ate, smiled and just did things out of the ordinary can be seen in my grandchild's actions.

FROM THE BEGINNING TO THE END

Brief Synopsis:

From the beginning to the end, all started quite a few years ago, when Josie decided to get married to Rudy Clark. The story begins with how she was as a little girl, and how her mom was a great inspiration in their lives growing up.

After marrying Rudy and starting their family, life began to crumble all around them, for more than 25 years of nothing but illness and disease and trauma going in their lives. The readers shall be blessed after reading their life story and how it will help the next family that is going through some hard times to keep on praying, the Father will indeed hear your prayers.

So as you read all of the chapters that is in this book, read with an open mind and stay prayerful. Everyone that read this book, it is not meant for you to go through the same things, but just a blessing to know how that our God is still on the Throne.

Be Blessed the Saints of the Most High God.

JOSEPHINE CLARK

Chapter 1

FROM THE BEGINNING TO THE END:

It was spoken by Yahweh God to his wife Josephine over some of 39 years ago, that it was Yahweh God destiny for Rudy to be save at the end. Not really knowing what this meant to Josie, she just obeyed God and married Rudy, in spite of what his past looked like. Not even knowing that Rudy had been raped by his uncles and friends starting at the age of 5 until he was about 9 years old. Not only then was it his uncle there was cousins that joined in also when was he 8 years old.

These things was repeatedly happen until it made him become a hustler when he was a teenager. Life became very hard for Rudy to adjust after they were married. Knowing the prayer life of Josie, made things for them a little better.

The story began, as you will read how from the beginning to the end came about. Rudy at the end was saved; this was the purpose Yahweh ordained for Josie to marry Rudy so he will be saved.

This is dedicated to all of you that know Yahweh God when He spoke to you and told you to do something that everyone else did not agree with you on. Your family members may not comprehend the reason, but obey God. You be encouraged to continue on in prayer, holding that person up to our Heavenly Father that at the end he/she will make it in.

JOSEPHINE CLARK

Chapter 2

HOW THEY MET

Their miracles began one year later, born unto Rudy and Josephine was their first daughter, Felecia and then the second one, Valorie. Her husband prophesied to Josephine, quote; we will be married before this year is out, this was July 1967.

Let's back up a little, Josephine and her husband had only been married three (3) months. They wanted to have children's' right away. Strange isn't it; only married for three months and want to have a child, not knowing whether you will remain married or not. Their belief is; when you said yes to marriage vows, you said yes to sin, sickness, and disease and in health, for richer or poorer and for better or for worse, but if one of these happen we are ready to checkout of the marriage.

Now after they were married, they began going to the doctor for check-ups to see if she could have children. How did she know she could not have children, easy, it was stated by her mom that she would not have children because she was born barren, no ovaries are tube to carry the children through, and therefore, she did not even have a monthly cycle till later on in life.

So while traveling back and forth to the doctor, Josephine and her husband spent well over $2000.00 dollars to hear the same things over and over again. Joshua said, "Whose report do we believe, we will believe the report of the Lord God Jehovah.

Now they are attending a church name "Faith Temple Church of God in Christ ", a man of faith that taught "have faith in God" every Sunday night. Any one that needs a miracle gets in line. Rudy and Josephine got in line and the pastor ask, what do you two want God to do? "They said we want a baby". The question was asked, "Do you believe God"? They said yes we do. The man of God laid hands on them and said go believing God for your miracle. Of course you know exactly what the man of God meant, go take care of business. LOL. Praise father Yahweh, three months after the time they received prayer Josephine got pregnant.

Let's back up, for the reason of prayer. When Josephine was a little girl, her mom knew that Josephine would not have children. Her monthly was not there, and the doctor had already spoken to her mom she will not have children unless a miracle was performed. Josephine was born without ovaries and there was no way to hold children in her body.

The miracle began: Josephine first encounter was to go to the doctor and see what was going on; there were no symptoms of pregnancies of any other symptoms there. So what made her think she was pregnant? Good question. At church Josephine has heard someone testimony, how God blessed her to get pregnant after having a major operation, because of cancer in the uterus. After that they went to see the doctor just to hear, I'm sorry Mrs. Clark you are not pregnant, and I don't see how you ever will, there is nothing there to hold a baby, you are barren.

"What a shock to hear such words". Do you think that stopped their faith from believing in God? NO! To their surprise, Josephine husband who did not know anything about miracles raised up in catholic background, not knocking catholic belief, stated, "We must believe if we want this baby."

Now the time has passed and it is now six months, I guess too soon to find out still if Josephine is pregnant. She should by now be three months, enough time to find out. They go to the doctor again and see what is going on. Same remarks from the doctor, no Mrs. Clark you are not pregnant and as I stated before there is nothing there to hold a baby. The doctor said well let me take some blood sample, urine and see if something is going on. Nothing showed through the blood or urine. They went home still disappointed about the results. Rudy and Josie now said it is time we really get on our knees and pray on one accord for this miracle. Rudy led the prayer and Josie was in agreement that the next time they go to the doctor they will see she is pregnant. They prayed for a girl to be born on their anniversary day. Three more months later they return to the same doctor, by this time Josie should be about six months. Doctor once more said no you are not pregnant; there were no symptoms or morning sickness. How could this be possible, remember God said all things are possible if ye only believe. Did they actually believe God was going to give them a child, absolutely? They returned home and still not understanding things that are happening to me. The doctor once again said no, maybe you have a tumor. They did not receive such negative words. The word of Yahweh states in Matthews 17:20 " And Jesus said unto them, Because of your unbelief; for verily I say unto you, If ye have faith as the grain of a mustard seed, ye shall say unto this mountain, remove hence to yonder place; and it shall remove", and nothing shall be impossible unto you". The mustard seed being the smallest seed among all seeds. Their faith needs only the smallest amount for an operation.

They were entering into their 7 months of pregnancy, when the decision was to return to the doctor once again for confirmation of her pregnancy. But to their surprise, this time the doctor ordered blood and urine test to be done in the office. To their surprise, there was something showing up in the blood which seems like she may be pregnant. The test returned positive and the doctor did not want to believe she was. The doctor said she was 6 weeks, but how could that be when she went from 95 lbs. to 130 lbs. So after the doctor tested her again and saw she was more that 6 months pregnant, the doctor wanted to know how many months she was. Josephine at that time was about 7 or 8 months, because of the movement of the baby. At that time they were leaning on the hands of the Lord. The doctor gave her prenatal care and ten stated the baby should be born around March or April, which was way off to be 8 months into the pregnancy. Rudy told the doctor the baby will be born December 16, the day they married on. The doctor thought Josephine was only 5 months but instead 8 months. The last of November labor pain began, but the baby would not come. Josephine suffered pains for about another month before doctor decided to take baby by way of operation. Josephine suffered a lot of pain and finally the doctor induced labor, for the baby, her head was not in the birth canal, her feet was coming first. By this time they had changed ministry and went to the pastor for prayer for the baby to turn into the right position. The ministry began to pray while Rudy and Josie stood in line, at that very instance of prayer the baby began to turn right in the eyes of the church. The pain was very bad and hurt for a long period of time.

Their baby girl (Felecia) was born to the Clark's on December 16, just as her husband stated she would. Just because their baby girl was born, did not mean everything was fine. She had been out of the water sack for at least 8 hours that when labor was induced. Since the baby girl is now here let's move on the next miracle Yahweh has performed for the Clark's.

JOSEPHINE CLARK

Chapter 3

BEGINNING OF THEIR FAMILY

Felecia is now crawling around and getting into everything. By the time she was 9 months, she could talk, holding conversation. They believe this was because during the time of pregnancy, her mom read every day to her while rubbing her stomach, because it was told words will form out of the baby mouth when she began to talk, she already has a vocabulary of words. Everything was going fine until Josie found out she was pregnant again with their second child. Their daughter Felecia made the way for the second child to be born because of her not being able from the beginning to have children. Praise Father Yahweh for that miracle.

A whole lot of action going on: their second child Valorie is born in August, a year ½ later. Their oldest daughter Felecia was about 1 year 8 months old, when the family was sitting down watching television and eating popcorn. Felecia thought her baby sister could eat popcorn; therefore she climbed into Valorie's bed and tried to feed her popcorn. To their surprise Valorie started choking which made the parents realize Felecia was in the bed with her sister. When Felecia called out saying baby is sick, they ran to her rescue, picked her up turned her over and lightly tapped her on the back, the popcorn came out. Rudy and Josie began to explain to Felecia that the baby is too young to eat popcorn. What happens next, Valorie is now about 8 months holding on to the end table trying to catch Felecia running around the table. So when Valorie reached to catch Felecia, she took off walking behind her trying to play. Valorie stopped walking at the time she reached 12 months. She was taking to the doctor to see what was going on. The doctor wanted to say it was a form of "Spinal Meningitis", not knowing how this happen. They prayers of the righteous availeth much. After the saints prayed for her, along with Rudy and Josie, another time God stepped in.

PRAISE FATHER YAHWEH:

Another time for the miracle working power of God: one Sunday morning they were preparing to go to church, they lived in an apartment on the south side of Chicago. The apartment had that old time fashion radiator, where you put water into the radiator to keep the heat regulated. Rudy turned the knob counter clock wise on the radiator to turn the heat down. They did not realize Felecia was watching, so as soon as Rudy left the room, Felecia went behind him and turned the knob, water came shooting out of the radiator, hit Felecia on the left side of her face and chest, the water were so hot you could see her flesh. They did not know what to do but pray, they made a phone call to the pastor of their church, and the pastor told them to use the anointing that had been placed on their lives through the Holy Ghost. They began to hold hands and pray for a miracle to take place. The pastor told them to pray and come to church. As they continue to get prepared for church, wrapped up Felecia, became obedient to the man of God and went to church. By the time they arrived at church, carried Felecia to the front of the church and unwrapped the blanket and Felecia has received a miracle from Yahweh. The pastor asked what happen, they were so overjoyed, could not even speak of what the father had done; the whole church began to praise God for such a miracle. The living proof was a scar on her chest to show she had been burned. WHAT A MIRACLE.

Time is now really moving right along, the girls are now entering school and Josie was at work part-time, they hired a baby sitter to watch the girls until Rudy get home from work around 5pm. The girls were around 6 and 8 years old. Felecia was playing carrying her sister on her neck. Valorie fell backward, hit her head on the basement floor and became partially blind. They called Josie and Rudy to come home. By the time they got home and wanted to rush Valoire to the emergency room. The pastor was called to pray, but these are the words that Valoire spoke to her mom. "Mom, stop crying and pray". By the time they got to the emergency room, the doctor stated because Valorie was very calm and didn't get upset was why she will not be blind , but for some hours and not totally blind forever.

Chapter 4

Another Exciting Episode:
STICK-UP TIME

Rudy was in the living room in the apartment watching television, when Josie came home from attending night class. When their apartment was broken into. It happen so fast they did not realized what happen. Suddenly there was a knock on the door, not realizing that Josie forgot to put the bolt on the door when she came in, therefore the door was not lock. Four young men, well dressed came into their apartment; each had a gun and rope. Rudy was in the floor eating popcorn, the girls in their room watching TV and Josie had gone into the bedroom. After the guys had come in, these are the words they spoke, "THIS IS A STICK UP". They didn't know what to do, but let the guys take whatever they wanted, just doesn't kill them. Josie decided to make a quick phone call to the security guard, who was downstairs. One of the guys saw Josie on the phone and made her get off, but the security guard had heard the man say this is a stick up and security called the police. By the time the policeman arrived, they were gone. One of the guys tied Rudy up in a knot; one had a shot-gun over the girls and one in the bedroom with the wife. They were searching for money and jewelry, but there was none. The guy that was in the bedroom with the girls told them if they don't stop crying, he would blow her brains out of the window. After all of this Felecia suffered emotional trauma, Valorie suffered with 6 ulcers , Rudy had several strokes, but with Josie nothing happen to her, because she was the one praying and talking to the guy, telling him he is not a murder. The girls at this time were 9 and 11 years old. Praise God for his blessing.

Another exciting episode:

By the time Valorie was about 12 years old and was trying to cook on the stove, the water in the pot was boiling and Val tired to move the pot, but instead dropped the pot on her foot, now burning her leg and floor, you could see her flesh. This time when they were called they did not take her to the hospital but applied some "anointing oil" to her foot. What makes this so special, the oil is prayed over for a point of contact with the father; it's all according to your faith.

Hallelujah, Praise God, Val received another miracle, the redness left, blisters left and her foot was only sore for a short time. Yahweh God is still working miracles.

It is now time for the girls to start going to High School. This is at the time Valorie always complain about going to class. She always stated her headache. What do we do as parents, they always say you just don't want to go to school but you are going today. This particular day , Josie took Valorie to school complaining about headaches, since she had been complaining for some time, it was another day she did not wanted to go to class. By the time she got to school, they received a phone call from the principle and stated that Valorie had passed out and the ambulance was called. The school rushed Val to the hospital at Michael Reese. Rudy and Josie met them at the hospital; they had already rushed her to do tests on her, because of the permission that was given over the phone to run tests while they were on their way. To their surprise the hospital discovered Valorie did not have enough blood in her system and needed a blood transfusion to live. Reason was she had "6 Ulcers." They wanted to give her a transfusion, of-course they refused. The hospital explained if anything happen while Val was in the hospital they would not be responsible for her death. They understood the policy of the hospital, but God was in control not the doctors. The doctors put Val on an intravenous feeding until the next morning hoping that mom would let them give her that transfusion. Josie spent the night at the hospital, praying all night for God to give her another miracle. Josie laid in the bed with Valorie talking to Yahshua, to her surprise, around midnight it seems as if Josie felled into a deep sleep and could not wake up till the nurse came into the room and woke them up so she can check on Val. To the nurse surprise, she took another test on Val and found out she had the amount of blood needed to live. The nurse thought someone had given her blood during the night. Oh yeah, she did receive blood but not from the doctors. Yahweh God sent His angel to do the job. The angel of the lord had come into the room and worked a miracle for her. Valorie did not have a blood transfusion; she had received a miracle during the midnight hour. WHAT A MIRACLE.

Now time is swiftly moving, the girls are out of school and everything seems to be working out fine. No more illness for them.

JOSEPHINE CLARK

Chapter 5

WHAT A TURN AROUND IT IS.

About 1986, life began to change again, this time it was the husband turn, they had been married around 19 years when these afflictions began. Their marriage was on the rock, their daughter Felecia was married and Valorie is married to Glenn Jr. Rudy had an operation to remove an abnormal urethra. After that he had 2 belly hernia removed. The next thing they knew he was having one hernia after another removed. They do not know why and where they were coming from. Once Rudy had another hernia removed, no one knew what happen in the hospital; (Name Unknown) Rudy ended up with an infection and was on an IV for about 9 months. Just to say no one knew what to expect next, but one thing for sure Rudy pulled through. While he was on the IV, Rudy wanted to get in the bath tub, as he was attempting to get out of the water, he slipped and the IV came out where there was incision in his side to drain out the poison, it came out with blood and water. One thing we are reminded of; when Jesus was pierced in His side out came blood and water for the remission of sin. Not saying this for Rudy, but now we know Jesus had to be here in the flesh. The tub began to fill up with blood; there was not enough time to call for the nurse this was not her day to be there. The only thing Josie could think of was to grab a towel and hold it tight to his side to stop the bleeding and pray. Yahweh God came through.

Another time Rudy wanted to go to church, the IV came

out again, this time Apostle was up preaching and laid hands on him and commanded the bleeding to stop. Immediately the bleeding stopped. Praise Yahweh, he made it again. Then Rudy began to feel different in his body regarding the pain he was feeling and could not explain. Sometimes in life we just ignore signs that tell us to go see a doctor; we push them aside because after a couple of days we feel better. After that Rudy heart became weak later on they found out he had a stroke, he became paralyzed on one side, and his memory was gone for about 6 months. Rudy could function a little at work, but did not know anything at home. He did not recognize his wife and he thought he was living in someone else home. Rudy was just out of it; his wife had to sleep in another room until all of this boiled over. Living in this situation brought on some unbearable situations. It took Rudy about 9 months to totally recover from his stroke. Yahshua came through again.

WHAT HAPPENS NEXT

Rudy suffered another sickness, he came down with a liver disease, his heart began to get weak, fluid started building up in his spleen, legs starts to swell, they went to the doctor, Rudy was told he had an infectious disease. They started going to University of Illinois Medical Hospital for treatment from the heart doctor and GI doctor. Fluids were filling so rapidly that they were seeing the doctor to drain that fluid every three (3) to four (4) weeks. The saints kept praying and Josie had put Rudy on some vitamins that were supposed to help him. A multi vitamin, calcium, E, A, B-complex. Omega 3 and several other that would help. So one day it all start to happening, the buildup of the fluid began to slow down little by little. If you ever see a little skinny man with a belly bigger than Santa, that was Rudy. After they had gone to the GI doctor for about three years, Rudy received a miracle, the fluid stopped building up, but his liver was still hard as a brick. Rudy lived like that until they moved. Now they are living in South Elgin, Rudy pasturing the church, members seeing him go and come. Prayers of the righteous availeth much. This was a time in their lives everyone wanted to move away. The south as Rudy called it was calling him to be there. The statement he made was "I want to die in Alabama". Rudy never lived in Alabama and did not know anything about living in the south. Since this is where he wanted to be, it was time to pack up and move. So in July 2003, they began the process to move to Alabama. They thought everything was going good for some reason, Rudy was doing well, his sickness had just completely left her mind, no doctor was being seen, and Josie had slowed down on giving Rudy those vitamins.

JOSEPHINE CLARK

Chapter 6

BEGINNING OF THE WORSE

Beginning at that time, Josie decided she was going to get a job at Wal-Mart on the second shift. One evening, she came home and found some of her neighbors in their apartment, in the bedroom with Rudy. He was vomiting, he had a temperature of 110 and he had to be rushed to the hospital. His vital signs were taken, but they didn't admit him to the hospital. They did not find anything major with him. Josie kept on working, Rudy got ill again, and this time he was rushed to the hospital and stayed about five days, still not understanding what was going on with his body. Rudy started having leg cramps, fingers cramping, he needed something to help him with cramps. They poured vinegar on his fingers and leg which usually stops the cramps. They asked the doctor about some pills to help him; the pill was in the form of Quinine. Now Rudy had been on this medication for about two years when they discovered there was another problem that is going on in his life, his PLATELETS were being destroyed along with a swollen spleen and cirrhosis of the liver. Cirrhosis is a disease that causes irreversible scarring to the liver, on top of this a diabetic in which they have high levels of sugar in the blood. Not only that Rudy immune system was under attack. (The immune system protects the body from invasion of foreign substances, such as bacteria and viruses and from cancerous cells). Rudy ended up with Jaundice, a yellowing of the skins and eye that is caused due to excessive bile products in the blood stream.

While in the hospital, this time Rudy is under another attack, he stopped eating, blood sugar racing high, how he is going through all of this and still have a desire to live and do the will of God.

Around March 2004, they traveled to Chicago first to visit Rudy's dad. Rudy was doing fine at least they thought. While in Maywood for two days, then decided to go on to Wisconsin to be with their daughter Valorie and grandchildren, but while there Rudy started doing a lot of coughing, he was rushed to Kenosha Medical Center where he stayed for four days. That is when they learned from the Medical Center that Rudy needed TIPS, because of the excessive ascites of fluid that is built up in the abdomen. The Medical Center in Kenosha could not perform the operation because Rudy specialist GI doctor had to perform, since they were only visiting. In June 2004, the operation was set and performed and the excess fluid stopped building up. (The TIPS are a stem-like straw that is inserted into the body that surpasses or placed as an extension from the liver to empty the fluid buildup which makes Rudy urinate more frequently). Before the operation the fluid buildup was excess amount urine that could not pass through the liver, therefore, it build up in the stomach area. This was the side effect of the leg and hand cramps.

While in Wisconsin, they visited Valorie and the family for Christmas. They arrived there on the 20th of December, to their surprise Rudy ended up in the hospital on the 21st of December, where the grandchildren, Valorie and Josie stayed in the room with him till 9pm. The trip back to Valorie house was the doctor did not tell us what is going on with Rudy. Since Rudy was still in the hospital, they wanted Rudy home for Christmas. It started to snow, they heard it was going to be a snow storm and the highways may be blocked. Two days later Rudy and Josie decided to start back home to Alabama. Rudy took ill again on the highway, vomiting and coughing, several times Josie had to pull off the highway for Rudy. On the way, they stopped at Rudy's dad home to get money to spend the night at a hotel because of the snow. Early the next morning they started again to go home, Rudy still vomiting, and all Josie could do was pray and ask God for strength to make it home. When they did arrive, Rudy wanted to go straight to bed and not to the hospital. The next day Rudy went to the hospital and found out he had been a diabetic for more than four months, was the reason for the vomiting.

Chapter 7

A MARK V111 - LINCOLN FAMILY REUNION

By this time Rudy doing good, eating right, on medication and able to control his blood sugar. Time and Time again Rudy was rushed to the hospital for some reason or another. They took another trip to Chicago where Rudy had a car that was being repaired. They thought before they left Illinois that the car would be ready and they could drive it to Alabama. Since they were not able to bring the car, there was another trip to Illinois. By July 2005, Rudy and Josie returned to Illinois to get his Lincoln. While returning on Highway 65 South, they got close to entering Indianapolis where they enter the turn to go to Kentucky, Rudy got lost on 65, Rudy felt as if those turns was a little too much. Josie pulled over on 65, waiting to see if she saw Rudy coming around the curve. Josie sat about 30 minutes and started to pray. Soon she could see Rudy slowly coming toward her, he knew the car and knew that was the one on the side. When Rudy got close, he pulled off the highway near her and told her he was afraid and started to drive real slowly, he could not see well after that. So as they continue down the highway, they drove very slowly with their hazardous lights on from Kentucky to Alabama. WHAT A BLESSING, YAHWEH GOD BROUGHT THEM THROUGH AGAIN.

Family Reunion

The reunion was held at their home in Huntsville,

Alabama, July 7-9-2005 Family members from all over came to the reunion. Rudy was trying his best to be happy, but most of the time, stayed back in the house out of the way of people. Rudy began to tell Josie, this will be my last time with all of the family, they will not see me after this event is over. Josie kept saying to Rudy, babe, don't say that, you will be around for a while; it is not your time.

Around August 2005, Rudy condition became worse; Rudy returned to the hospital and stayed about four days. After different medication, Rudy started feeling better, going out to dinner, able to walk without a walker and doing well. After that, Rudy returned back to the hospital several times, from October to December 2005. Rudy went to the hospital, December 26, 2005 about 5pm to receive platelets and blood. (Platelets mean it is a colorless dislike body of mammalian blood that is derived from fragments of megakaryocytic cytoplasm, that is released from the bone marrow into the blood, and that assists in blood clotting by adhering to other platelets and to damaged epithelium, also called blood platelet). On the 28th of December, Josie wanted to know how much blood they were going to give Rudy. This time it was around 8:45am, she had not yet received any information as to how much blood he would get. Around 4pm, the nurse came to draw blood to see what type is needed. This is the second day Rudy is in the hospital without medical attention, blood count getting lower and lower.

Now around 9:10 pm on the 28th of December, the nurse came to give Rudy platelets and blood. One thing Josie noticed is when the beeper went off on the machine that was dispensing blood, the nurse was called to come to adjust it, it took them about 7 minutes before coming in the room. This time Rudy stayed in the hospital from December 1st, 2005 to January 6th, 2006. (Platelets are very tiny blood cells that will help stop the bleeding in the body, by binding together a clump or plug site of injury inside of the blood vessels. The normal blood count is about 150,000 to 450,000 platelets per MCL. Within men the normal count is 237,000 MCL and women 266,000 MCL). Platelets are usually produced in the marrow of the bones.

Rudy returned again on the 15th of January, 2006 Rudy went into a deep sleep, feet yellow under the bottom, even the doctor could not awake him; NO SUCCESS. His blood sugar read 253, pulse and heart beat, blood pressure reading 118, 80, 76, ammonia level 102 , blood 35 and platelets 29. This was pretty good according to his doctor, with him in this condition. Rudy stayed about 6 days and woke up, and was released on the 21st of January.

Chapter 8

RUDY'S LAB RESULTS

Now Josie decided to take good care of Rudy at home. While Rudy was at home the ammonia in his body got extremely high, because of not taking his lactose three times a day, the amino acid will go up. During that time the therapist had started coming to house to check on Rudy. This was set up by the hospital since he is being cared for at home. The therapist comes three times a week to assist Rudy with walking, feeding, bathing and taking his medicine. The nurse came on Monday's to draw blood and to check his platelet level, and amino acid level. The nurse called the hospital and requested Rudy needed to be admitted again, his platelets were low around 60,000. Rudy returned to the hospital on the 26th of January 2006 after being home for a very short time. This time Rudy went into a COMA, and stayed until 3rd February 2006. His walking is now more and more difficult. Rudy was released on the 3rd and returned on the 6th of February. While Rudy was in the coma, the nurse gave him a shot so he will rest; he seemed to be restless even in a coma. Nurse K. was asked to give Rudy a bathe since he had not had a bathe from 10:30am to 5pm on the 11th of February. Rudy started coughing real hard; it was mention to the nurse so it could be recorded in the report.

Rudy complained of stomach pain, while in a coma, how Josie knew this. Rudy kept rubbing his stomach and groaning. They placed Rudy in CCU2, the male nurse did not mention it to the doctor they only gave him a shot to keep him from being restless from 10th of February to 12th of February. After that Rudy was placed in a regular room and Josie stayed there until visiting hours were over. The doctor had to ask Josie to go home and get some rest, but she would only return the early the next day. Rudy stayed wet from 2:00am till 6:30am until nurse K and nurse J came in the room and wanted to know how Rudy was doing. Josie mentions he has not opened his eyes since the 10th. When Josie mention to Nurse K and nurse J to make sure the doctor know Rudy is coughing a lot. Then nurse K stated "as long as I mention it to the doctor that's all I can do". Radiologist came into the room to put a pick-line in his arm, in order not to keep sticking him to get blood and any other lab treatment. As soon as Josie came back in to the room the pick-line was bleeding, nurse K claim Mr. Clark must have pulled on it to bleed, and how could he if he is in a deep sleep? This was around 8:00am that morning, now it is 11:45am before someone else came to check the bleeding. In which Rudy had excessive bleeding in his brain and it needed to be stopped. Wow, what a mess, no one wants to do their job correctly, just let a person bleed because you know they are dying.

On the 14th of February, the doctor thought it would be best for Rudy to be placed on a nutrimental diet, since he had to travel later on in February to UAB in Birmingham for more extinctive lab work. Rudy lips were dry and had some small blister on them; tears started streaming down his face, frowning because of the pain. The doctor seeing Rudy ammonia around 161 and have not had a bowel movement, his ammonia was climbing higher. On Wednesday morning, Rudy was transferred to UAB in Birmingham. The ambulance arrived 7:15pm and arrived at UAB at 8:45pm. After being placed in a room, nurse came in to take S.T.A.T.S. now his ammonia is now 234. On Thursday there was no talking with Rudy, eyes closed and lips very dry. The nurse on night shift was an excellent person; communication toward Josie meant a lot. Rudy was given some lactose through the rectum so he could have a bowel movement. This needed to happen so the doctor could really see what was going on in the body. Rudy was snoring hard every night, coughing, moving all over the bed with the pick-line in his arm. CT-Scan was done to make sure no blood was in his brain. "Rudy please wake up is Josie cry". The nurse came into the room and gave him another shot to help ease the pain and to change his dressing. The doctors thought Rudy was able to receive a LIVER TRANSPLANT. After arriving in Birmingham, the stay was 14 days. More and more test was done to see if his body was strong enough for this transplant. To their surprise, he could not get a transplant, but there was no liver for him. Rudy liver was damaged badly, cirrhosis of the liver, all started over 21 years ago from an operation Rudy received from some dirty tools the hospital used, to remove some abnormalities in his body. After several testing, there was nothing that could be done for Rudy, so UAB returned him back to Huntsville.

Rudy was sent home, family members were called, along with his daughters. Rudy's condition was getting worse. His daughter Valorie was able to come and spend a couple of days with him. She laid in the bed, feed him and stayed by his side for those two days. Rudy's dad and sister came also. To their surprise, Rudy did not know they were there in the room with him. On Monday Rudy returned back to the hospital.

Josie left the hospital on Thursday night 16th of February, because of the leaders coming down from Illinois was on their way to visit. They arrived on Friday, they all came to the hospital around 3pm and stayed about an hour, prayed and left. Rudy still has not talked since the 9th of February. Today the 18th of February, the ones from Illinois began their journey back home. Josie returned to the hospital to stay with Rudy and stayed there until Sunday morning, so she left the hospital and went to church so she could pray the will of God in her life and Rudy. Sunday morning Josie went to Jasper where her nephew is the pastor. The pastor sent home with her some communion to give to Rudy even though he was in a coma. The communion was placed on a sponge and placed on Rudy tongue. Hallelujah Praise Father Yahweh was the words from the pastor, RUDY IS COMING OUT.

On the 18th of February nurse L came into the room to put some tape on Rudy arm to help keep the pick-line in properly. Josie asked nurse L should she use some gauge first to keep tape from pulling off the skin. Nurse L stated, I don't have to use any gauge because the bleeding was cleaned off previous blood. Then Josie mentions to nurse L, she wanted to talk to the nurse in charge to see if that was correct. Nurse L said," that's fine plus the sheets from last night has not been changed also, be sure to tell her that". The nurse in charge did not come in until 9:50pm when her shift started at 7:30pm to answer my question. What Josie mention to nurse in charge is "does this hospital promoted customer service to their patient or not? What Josie expressed to nurse in charge, was that nurse L pulled the tape off and had Mr. Clark crying because of the pain and he started to bleed again.

Today is now 22st of February, 2006 and one brother in Christ stayed all night while Josie went home to get some rest. The doctor came in the next morning when Josie returned and said, Mr. Clark is still sleep. The doctor clapped his hand and said," Mr. Clark wake up and open your eyes. What a joy Rudy opened his eyes and began to say Praise God and the only thing Josie could say was, Praise Father Yahweh for opening Rudy's eyes.

JOSEPHINE CLARK

Chapter 9

QUOTES OF RUDY AFTER WAKING UP

4th of February: Valorie the daughter ask, "Daddy are you ready to die?"

Answer: "Course not."

5th of February: Rudy was quiet, eyes closed, and Valorie was sitting on the edge of the bed. Rudy said in a strong voice "JESUS IS THAT YOU, HELLO, HELLO."

10th of February: Rudy saying, "let's go to the River, listen Jo I have a lot to tell you."

13th of February: Rudy spoke to the brother in the room, "Man turn off that Television."

Then Rudy said, "Jo do you know Sarah, have you seen Sarah? I'm tired of Alabama."

These quotes were being said while Rudy was in a coma, just talking away at home. Why Josie did not take him to the hospital at that time was his request before he stopped talking. Rudy told Josie, "I will let you know the right time to take me to the hospital."

Quotes when Rudy woke up

22st of February: "Please take this thing out of my nose."

This was the first thing he mentioned after being asleep for 18 days. "Then when can I go home?"

23rd of February: "Jo I have a lot to tell you when I get out of this place."

24th of February: "Doctor O, do you know I seen the LORD?" "O yes Mr. Clark, I know you don't want to believe it, because I know how the weather is going to be."

"Jo I went down deep, real deep and I had to come back to talk to you."

"I was in a low place and I need to come up to the 1st floor, where I can rest. Jo it seems like you were in a hole and I was trying to get you."

2st of March: "Jo get in touch with an Airline for tickets, fly now and pay later, you are about to get real busy."

2st of March: Rudy blood sugar has been normal for a while, 105, 97, and 162 and was doing pretty good.

Chapter 10

WEATHER PREDICTION

Today is the 24th of February a Thursday morning and Rudy had not been to the bath room in a minute. The laxative that was given to him was supposed to be working. The dosage was increased tremendously from 20cc's to (3X) a day to 120cc's. This was given at 3:30pm and now it is 9:30pm and stills nothing. Rudy's body must be under so much stress that his blood sugar is even up high today. (ON THE THIRD DAY YASHUSHA AROSED FROM THE GRAVE). His nephew sent communion to the hospital to administer to him, and they tell you on the third day after putting communion on a sponge and giving it to him, Rudy open his eyes and said "I need my clothes to go home." The doctor told him as soon as you get better you can go home. Josie was not in the room when he opened his eyes; she came in and saw Rudy lying on his side. Josie ran out of the room and going to each nurse station saying, "My husband is alive, my husband is alive, his eyes are open". Rudy had been sleep for 18 days. This was the day Rudy was going to Birmingham again to get a re-evaluation for a transplant.

This morning the 25th of February nurse P asked Mr. Clark how are you feeling to today, answer was; "I'm feeling just fine; she said are you sure? Mr. Clark said, "absolutely".

Monday afternoon, the 27th of February around 1:30pm, Josie arrived to help finish feeding and bathing Rudy for the nurse. They are glad when Josie comes because Rudy refused to let them bathe him because he wanted his wife. The therapist came around 2pm to take him walking, change his dressing and take his S.T.AT.S. Today Rudy is little more alert than usual and he is feeling better and talking a lot. Doctor O came in the room, and Rudy asked; "doctor did you know I saw the Lord" well is what the doctor said. Rudy then said, "I don't care if you believe me or not, I know I seen the Lord", and He is going to change the weather". Jo there is a great change coming in the weather. Josie went back and checked on the weather for February 2006.

2006 weather summaries:

Assessments

These predictions were quoted before Rudy's death.

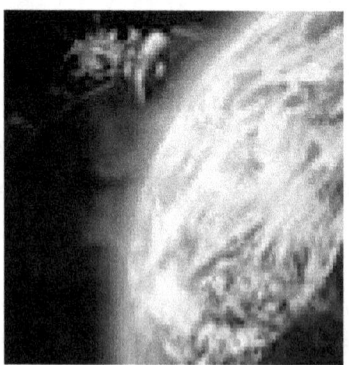

Tropical cyclone warning and tropical storm forecast around the world.

FROM THE BEGINNING TO THE END

2007 Weather Year in Review

Some of the pictures show how the weather changed in the year of 2007. Just to show how the prediction of what Mr. Clark spoke was true. Tropical cyclone which in tandem with a high pressure system to the north created a steep pressure gradient, strong winds, and monstrous waves.

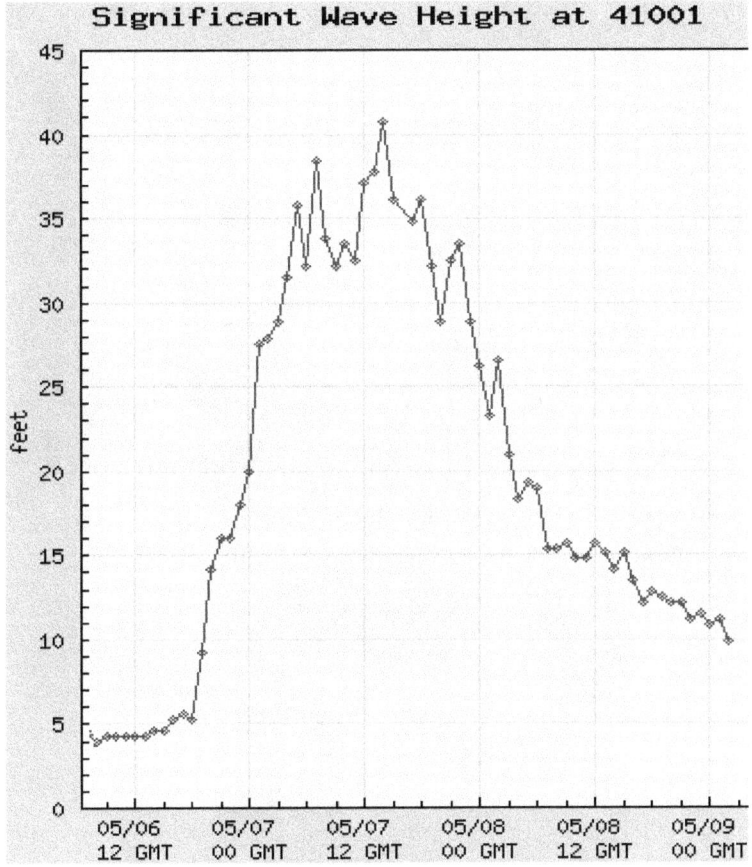

waves such as at this buoy:

45

With high winds and rain this became a subtropical-storm. Where this is the earliest in the season that there is a subtropical or tropical storm has directly affected the U.S.

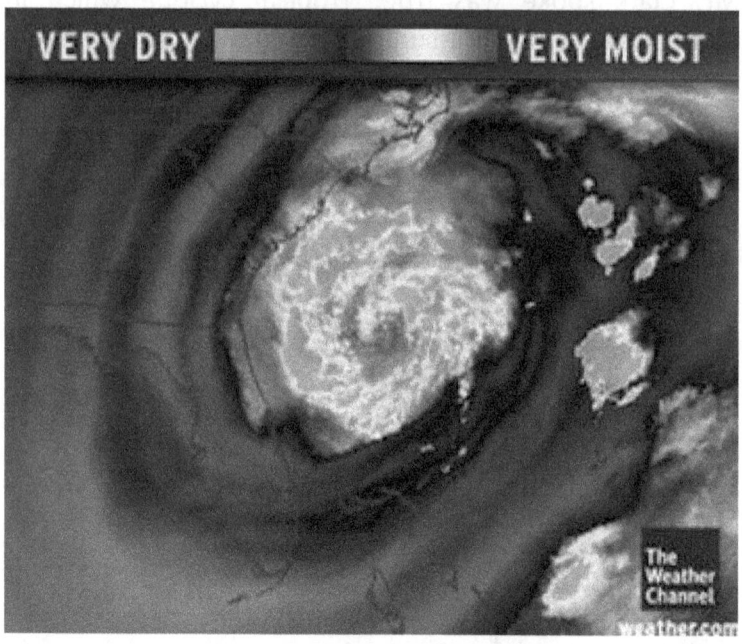

And then after weakening, its circulation drew in smoke from the wildfires in <u>parched</u> Georgia and Florida:

This is the first tornado in history for Southern Canada in late June to be rated as an F5. Where Elite, Manitoba (Canada has not yet adopted the new EF scale of the intensity of tornados.

While the very next day there was severe thunderstorms erupted in southern Canada again that includes a cyclic tornado super cell which moved from Saskatchewan into Elite Manitoba. You can see the tornado grow in size; darken and become dramatically contrasted with the backlight.

This is an unusual sight. With a close-up of the inner core of the tropical cyclone is so vivid -- although this one is particularly 3-D-ish, this sort of amazing-looking structure is often seen courtesy of high-resolution MODIS imagery when tropical cyclones become very intense. Nor is the second image out of the ordinary, this is the type known as a microwave image with meteorologists utilize nowadays.

What was unusual is that the Category 5 intensity in the first image was over the Arabian Sea, and at the time of the second one, Gonu was still of hurricane strength as it headed into the Gulf of Oman

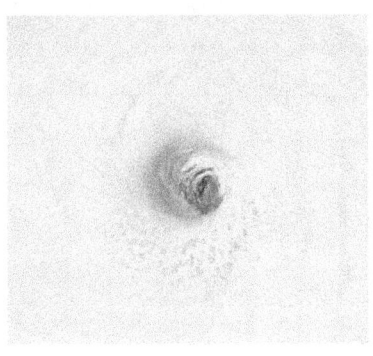

At one point Iowa received some blast repeatedly by heavy northwest flow thunderstorms, one of which produced this gigantic hailstone:

While the weather was stormy in July, there was some sizzling going on in Montana, and the heat transferred to many other states as August progressed.

Chapter 11

THE START OF SOMEHTING NEW

Then around 10:50pm Josie fell asleep, but was awakening by some stirring in the bed, Josie woke and to her amazement saw Rudy sitting on the side of the bed just resting. Now if she had said Rudy laid down he would ask why? I just want to sit up for a while. She did not even know he could sit up on his own. Rudy was a very strong man, when he wanted to he could pull him self up without any help.

Tonight nurse P came to give Rudy his shot of four unites based on last number numbers on the chart. The nurse stated she forgot to erase the board from the previous night. The tech did the reading at 12:15pm and did not have time to change the board. Then about 4am in the morning, Josie fell asleep again and this time after Rudy stopped talking. But that Saturday night nurse P called to get an alarm for Rudy bed because of the stirring so much. It would take three days to get one. Therefore, Josie still left without an alarm for Rudy. This time around 2 or 4 am in the morning, it happened, Rudy woke me up saying, "Jo help me, and help me Jo. Josie woke up and found Rudy face down on the floor; he had falling out of the bed. Josie asked him what happened; Rudy stated he was in the basement and trying to come up from the basement when he fell.

On 1st of March 2006, after Rudy had gotten his bathe, ate and sat up for a while. Then Rudy mention he saw an angel that was watching him and given him his number. Rudy stated he cannot tell what the angel was trying to explain to him. Then Rudy wanted to know if Jo can depend on him, Jo said yes.

Now today is 3rd of March and Rudy sat up for about 10 minutes. Rudy felt as if he was getting ready to do ministry again. He mentions that new people were coming because of the anointing in the ministry.

On 4th of March, Tan and Josie sister, Maggie came in from Birmingham to spend some time with Rudy; the song that Tan sang was "I see Jesus in you". Those very words put Rudy to sleep and it surely brought tears to Josie eyes. After they left the hospital Josie went home so she can prepare to go to church on Sunday. Rudy wanted her to go and not stay at the hospital. On 7th of March was the release day for Rudy, doing good and able to eat. The very next day was the beginning of their full day at home. Josie showed Rudy how to pull up on the side of the bed to sit up for a while each about 10-15 minutes at a time. Rudy learned how to use his walker so he can take that long haul down the hallway to the kitchen. On 9th of March, they could see a lot of progress going on. Rudy now can walk from the bedroom to the kitchen with no assistant from Josie. He could now brush his teeth, wash his face and hold the spoon to feed himself.

Today is now Friday 10th of March 2006; Rudy rolled over and felled out of the bed twice, all because he wanted the rails down. Rudy had been doing so well getting up and sitting on the side of the bed with the railing down. After that fall, 911 was called, they took Rudy to the hospital to make sure there was no bleeding. "Praise God our Father", everything was fine. They returned home around midnight, Rudy was ready to eat, so after eating they sat up for a while and went to bed. Now the 12th of March 2006, Rudy is trying so hard to feed himself. He also took a few steps such as get in the wheel-chair, walk along the wall to the bedroom. Then Steve came by to take him outside to get fresh air. "What a blessing to have someone that is willing to help carry the load." Today is now 26th of March, and Josie was preparing breakfast in the kitchen, so she ask Rudy to sit at the table and practice writing his name. During all of these processes, Rudy hand writing was gone.

One thing for sure Josie can say while Rudy was in the hospital from 5th of February to 7th of March. Brother W was there all of the time, looking after his buddy. When the ones from Illinois came down, Rudy had not been in the hospital for over 2 ½ weeks. Patton, Lofton, Kemp, Veronica, and a few others drove in to see their Pastor. What a prayer from Patton, Rudy bed began to shake as she prayed over his life. The anointing was what destroyed the yoke.

JOSEPHINE CLARK

Chapter 12

THE HANDWRITING ON THE WALL

This was done on March 26, 2006

This one was done on March 31, 2006

This one was done 04-01-2006

All of the photos were done while Josie was cooking breakfast. Josie was working on Rudy tying to keep his hand writing where it can be notice.

This one was done April 6, 2006

There is some evidence that Rudy writing was improving, around April. Everything seems to be improving, only for a season.

Today 2st of April, 2006, Rudy is able to do other things, such as feeding and making steps walking. He tried to walk without the walker and stays awake just a little longer than he has in the pass. On the 6th of April, Rudy walked outside with his walker to get in the car. Before they made the trip to the car, Josie and Rudy had prayer, asking Yahweh for more direction on what the step in their lives will be. When there is no direct answer from the Lord, it is best to leave things just the way they are. No answer, don't do anything, but keep believing, but it was already pre-destiny what the outcome will be.

Rudy spoke to Josie on the 13th of July, 2005 and told her the last day he will be in the earth was the 13th of July, 2006. He told her to prepare herself for this event and don't worry, Yahweh will take good care of you. Did it not happen that way? Yes it did. Praise is to God, who will not let you go blind to what he plan on doing. Today is the 10th of April, 2006. Rudy is sitting up eating breakfast, when Josie looked over and saw him shedding tears. When Josie asked what was wrong. Rudy said, "He was tired of people making promises about coming over to pray for her and let you go to church. They will not even call or they come over to late for Josie to go". When they come, Josie make some correction, they don't like it or don't show up anymore for weeks. Before then, they claim they love you, call to see if you need anything from the store, but when correction is made that's it. How can we say we love Yahweh when the scripture says," How dwelleth the love of Yahweh, when we see our brother or sister in need and we shut up our bowels of compassion." We must be sure where our love is.

Rudy's appetite is doing good, but Josie is concern because his health is seems to be changing. He has became depressed, weak, and even more confused than before, it is hard for Josie to work on keeping his bowels open. When she use to give him 4 dosage of lactose, now she has to give him approximately 8 to 9 dosage just to keep him open. Sometimes, when all of those dosages, especially when Josie is now guessing how much to give him in-order not to over-dosage. It maybe strange to everyone else, but not Josie, she only following orders from the doctor.

Lactose is 10ml/15ml high tech does not have any side effects until it reaches the colon, and since transit time through the colon may be slow, from 24 to 48 hours is required to produce a normal stool. So you see why it is given so often to produce a stool, because of time it takes to the colon.

Chapter 13

RUDY'S DEATH

On the 11th of April, 2006, Rudy had to be admitted to the hospital so he can go to UAB for more observations on his life. UAB was doing another evaluation since it was difficult for Josie to drive Rudy to Birmingham. While Rudy was being admitted, his ammonia went from 85 to 161 by Tuesday night. The nurse came into the room to give him a laxative, Rudy fell into a sleep coma. The dosage then was given at 9pm, 7am next morning, 2pm, and 7pm, and still there was no movement in his bowels. As soon as his bowels open, Rudy woke up.

On 15th of April, 2006, Rudy was going home; doctors finally stated there is nothing they can do to help Mr. Clark get a replacement. So from the 15th of April to the 23rd of April, Rudy seems to be doing ok. Time is really approaching from the time Rudy stated he will be going home, and what he meant was going home to be with the Lord. One day around the 24th of April, Rudy told Josie it is almost time to start preparing me for the hospital. It was time for the family reunion and Rudy could not go any place until the right time. Rudy finished doing a family portrait of all the sisters and their husband and their children and great-grandchildren; it was indeed a lot of work. Mr. Clark worked hard on finishing what no one else of thought, memories for years to come. Rudy had to be admitted to hospital, he became very ill and could not feed himself or even lift his head. The experience this time with Rudy in the hospital was quite different from all of the other times. Josie could actually say from the year 2005 to 2006, Rudy was in and out of the hospital so many times, she lost count. Rudy pressure was climbing higher each day with the help of some medicine, only to be careful not to give too much.

On the 2st of May till the 11th of May, 2006, Rudy pressure was decreasing more each day with the help of plenty fluids and other medicine. The doctor stated Mr. Clark can go home on the 12th if his pressure and eating habits were better. So Josie encouraged Rudy to eat and take his medicine so he can go back home. On the 12th of May, 2006 Rudy was discharged from the hospital and with a little help he walked with a walker and could spoon himself just a little. Josie went to the grocery store and brother W. came over to stay until she returns. In the meanwhile, Rudy and W. decided they will bake a cake. When Josie returned, flour, sugar, eggs and even milk was all over the place. The kitchens looked a hot mess and guess who had to clean up the kitchen? Josie. That Sunday the 12th, Rudy wanted to know can he go to church. Since Rudy can't sit in wheelchair that long or stay awake. Josie told Rudy next time she will try to make arrangement for him to go.

On the 13th till the 21st of May, 2006 Rudy wanted Josie to read to him stories out of the bible. Rudy medicine was costing a lot for him, so it was hard to keep fluids, pampers, bed pads, and other items that was needed to keep him comfortable. Thanks God for cousins that live close by that was willing to pitch in and help Josie out for the month. The Fords, they are very special to Josie.

So from 22st of May to 26th of May, 2006 Josie was able to do some-things that had not been done in a long time.

This time it is 2st of June, 2006 and Rudy was doing ok, not his best days, but ok. Later on that night he wanted Josie to leave the rails down, he promised her he would be good and not try to get out of bed. Josie listens, they went to bed and in the midnight hour, to her surprise, she kept hearing this cry, HELP ME HELP ME. Josie finally woke up and to her surprise, Rudy was under the bed had fallen out on the floor and could not move.

What was Rudy trying to go, he said walk around because he was not sleepy.

On the morning of 2st of June, 2006, Rudy began to feel time was close for him to return to the hospital. He did not want to die at home. That was fine, Josie thought it was better, because they could take better care of him if he died in the hospital. Rudy began to tell Josie it is now time for me to return to the hospital. I don't know what's wrong, but just get me admitted. So Josie got dressed and called for W. and E. to come and go with them to the hospital.

After Rudy was admitted, doctors were trying to figure out what's going on with him. It was the same thing over and over again; his kidney and liver had stopped functioning properly. The doctor wanted to know why he is here. Josie told doctor that Rudy said he felt real bad and wanted to be checked out by the doctor. Maybe the fall the other night made him feel bad. This was just time for Rudy to depart and be with his Heavenly Father, and he knew time was near.

On the 18th of June, Rudy still in the hospital and nothing is going on, blood pressure still high, and can't get it under control. Diabetes out of control, the more insulin they give him the worse he got. This was also the time the mortgage company asked me to move out of the house, because there was no money paid on the house for over 2 years. The mortgage company stated they were willing to work with me after finding out the condition of her husband. To her surprise after the mortgage company found out that she had limited amount of money she was told to move.

Now it is getting harder and harder, nurses and doctors keep coming into the room and wanted to know what going on. Rudy now have bed sores and they cannot send him home with bed sores. We don't know how quickly he got those sores, one thing for sure he was not going home with them. This was going on for some time now; nurses would clean him and treat him real bad, just to see a grown man cry was a hurting thing. Rudy slipped into a coma again around the 26th of June, and stayed like that till the 5th of July, 2006. Finally Rudy woke up and said, Josie I had to come back, I need to tell you something. Please get in the spirit so we can talk. Later on that night around midnight, Rudy started talking about how he needed to cross over Jordan River and did not know how to get there. Josie will you help me?

On the 6th of July, 2006 Rudy decided not to speak again, because he felt Josie was not listening to him. So later on the 10th of July, he started to speak again, this time Josie was ready to help him. He needed to cross over and it seemed as if he did not know how to. There was a door he needed to open and Josie was the only one that could open the door for him. Strange to say, after Josie open the door, Rudy said now I can go home, but before I do Josie, don't forget the insurance I took out for you over 30 years ago they will get in touch with you, don't worry.

So on the 13th of July, 2006, Rudy body had healed, no bed sores, blood pressure was very low, and his body temperature had dropped lower that the normal. Rudy began to say don't worry Josie I will be in a better place and I will always watch over you.

On the 14th of July, 2006, Rudy told Josie to go home; there is no need to stay with me any longer. Josie did not want to leave, she wanted to be there with him when he takes his last breathe, but instead she went home and told Rudy she will see him early the next morning. Josie went on home and around 3:00am the 15th of July the hospital called Josie. The nurse said Rudy parted this life around 2:30am, he is already clean, we left him in the room for your viewing; just take your time getting here.

It was a joy in taking care of Rudy, if she had to do it over, it would still be a joy to take care of the person that born her children. Such a joy just to know when your love one leaves, they've gone to a better place, just to be with their creator.

JOSEPHINE CLARK

Chapter 14

JOSIE'S NEW LIFE

One of the most strangest thing that happen to her right after the death of her husband, SSI had given her the money for the month, but after she called and reported his death, the very next 2 days, the money was taken back from SSI.

This was also the time the mortgage company asked me to move out of the house, because there was no money paid on the house for over 2 years. The mortgage company stated they were willing to work with me after finding out the condition of her husband. To her surprise after the mortgage company found out that she had limited amount of money she was told to move.

All of this took place after the death of Mr. Clark, a very hard and trying year for Ms. Clark to endure. She did not have any money and no place to go. So three months after still living in the house, Josie called the mortgage company again to see if there was a solution to help her stay in the house, and to her surprise there was no solution. The next morning Josie got up and called her daughter. She did not know Josie had to move out of the house and had no car to drive. Her daughter began to say in a demanding voice and told her to get up and go find yourself an apartment and get yourself a car.

Josie did not have any money for a down payment on a car or apartment. Talking about the favor of Yahweh, everything that was needed was in the press. Around

October 2006, Josie started out one morning walking to locate her place to live. The first place she went, the leasing manager was very nice, listens to her story and said she would run her credit to see if she qualifies without a deposit. Josie remembered what her daughter said, "Mom, pray as you look and believe Yahweh will open that door for you. She explained her situation and stated she will be able to pay as soon as her benefits were released. The manager stated it would be fine and that all she needed was 300 deposits.

The next day, Josie got up early and starts walking again to find her a car. She walked about 12 blocks, talking and praising Yahweh for answering her prayers. The first car lot she went to, she sat down and met with one of the managers from Illinois that had visited the church before and was now living in Alabama. Don't tell me, that Yahweh don't have everything already planned out for you, if you only trust him to do what He said He will do. PRAISE FATHER YAHWEH. To her surprise, Josie did not have a deposit but explained the same thing to the manager. As soon as her money is released she can come in with the deposit. This time the deposit was 1500. Do you think the manager let her drive off the lot with just a promise to return with 1500? YES, Josie showed them a promissory note for the money she will get. Josie drove off the lot and returned a month later with that deposit. Yahweh is still good. Josie had within two days of going out looking, apartment and a car.

Praise Yahweh for his love, care and tender mercy.

Chapter 15

FROM THE BEGINNING TO THE END OF IT SCRIPTURES AND HOW THEY STARTED

The starting point:

Genesis 1:1 St John 1:1-3	Creation
Genesis 3:1-6; Romans 5:12-21	Sin
Genesis 3:3, 22-24	Death
Ephesians 1:4	Salvation
John 8:44	Satan
Galatians 3:8	The Gospel
Ephesians 19:5; Jeremiah 31:31-34	The Old Covenant
Matthews 26:28; Hebrews 9:14-27	The New Covenant

The end of it:

Matthews 24:3, 14	Events Connected Day of Salvation
Matthews 13:36-43	Harvest of Souls
II Thessalonians 2:1-12	Defeat of Man of Sin
Matthews 25:31-46	Judgment
II Thessalonians 1:6-10	Destruction of the World

The coming of:

II Peter 3:3-5	Denied by Scoffers
Matthews 24:12	Preceded by Lawlessness
Luke 18:8	Preceded by Apostasy
Matthews 24:37-42	Without Warning
II Thessalonians 1:7-10	With Fire

Attitude Toward:

Matthews 25:1-13	Watchfulness
Matthews 25:14-30	Industry
Luke 21:25-28	Hopefulness
Romans 13:12-14; II Peter 3:11, 14	Holy Living
II Peter 3:9, 15	Seeking the Lost
II Peter 3:13; Revelation 22:1	Waiting for Eternity

JOSEPHINE CLARK

Special Photos

JOSEPHINE CLARK

JOSEPHINE CLARK

JOSEPHINE CLARK

JOSEPHINE CLARK

www.ingramcontent.com/pod-product-compliance
Lightning Source LLC
Chambersburg PA
CBHW060851050426
42453CB00008B/935